Keith Haring

I wish I didn't have to sleep!

Do you see that guy there on the left with the glasses?
Well, that's Keith Haring. In a moment we'll be taking a closer look at his
art and the many different things that his artwork involves. Also, we'll learn from
different kids what they think about when they see his art. But first a quick
question: What do you think is the most important thing to Keith in this picture?
Right! His sneakers, which get better the older and more worn out they are!
He always seems to have them on, whether with a T-shirt and jeans or a blue suit.

LET THE WORLD OUT THERE KNOW !

Keith Haring was always drawing pictures. Even as a young boy
he used to create short comics with his father and once he won a prize
at school for a comic he made. After graduating from high school in Kutztown,
Pennsylvania, where he grew up with his parents and three sisters, Keith
went to graphic design school in Pittsburgh, Pennsylvania, at the suggestion of his
parents. But Keith quickly discovered that he didn't want to make only
commercial designs, and that he liked making his own art even more. He was
interested in exploring his own imagination. When he was twenty years old, Keith
left Pennsylvania for the one place he felt was big enough for all the art
he wanted to make: New York City.

SUBWAY ART!

While he was an art student at the School of Visual Arts in New York City, Keith realized that he wanted to bring art to *everyone* rather than creating art only for museums or individuals. He wanted to work with lots of different people, inspiring their imaginations and emotions. The most important thing to Keith was to be able to communicate to the whole world.

One day, while riding the subway, Keith noticed the plain black paper hanging in all the unused advertising space. He ran to a store and bought plain white chalk, returned to the subway, and started drawing. Keith knew that he could get into trouble with the police if he was caught drawing on the paper, so he had to work fast. With just a few lines, his simple figures came to life. Sometimes they became barking dogs or a group of heads. Sometimes they became little characters hugging each other, pyramids, light bulbs and flying saucers. After drawing in the subway stations a few times, Keith had attracted a lot of attention. People often simply stood and watched him work, but sometimes they asked him what his drawings really meant.

He used to reply:

"It's your job to decide. I only do the drawing!"

SYMBOLS

Artists have different ways of letting others know a painting is theirs. They might sign it with their name or put a special symbol on it. Keith often drew a "Radiant Baby" as his signature on an artwork. The rays around the baby are not radioactive, they symbolize energy. Because Keith felt that art should be everywhere, he put drawings like the "Radiant Baby" on everyday items such as posters, buttons and T-shirts. But there are other images besides the "Radiant Baby" that Keith used again and again that are now recognized around the world. He also drew the "Barking Dog" and dancing people in different colors. By rearranging the same pictures in different ways, Keith was able to change the meaning and feeling of every picture.

Soon Keith was invited to paint on walls all over the world. Instead of getting into trouble for it, Keith was asked by city officials to paint murals! Sometimes kids helped him but, mostly, they just came to watch Keith work. They wanted to let him know that they liked what he was doing, and sometimes they asked him to draw on their T-shirts, jeans, and even on their shoes.

As Keith became more popular and well known, he still took the time to work with kids on projects that he felt were important. Keith designed a poster to encourage kids to read, painted an anti-drug mural, and donated art to raise money for AIDS research.

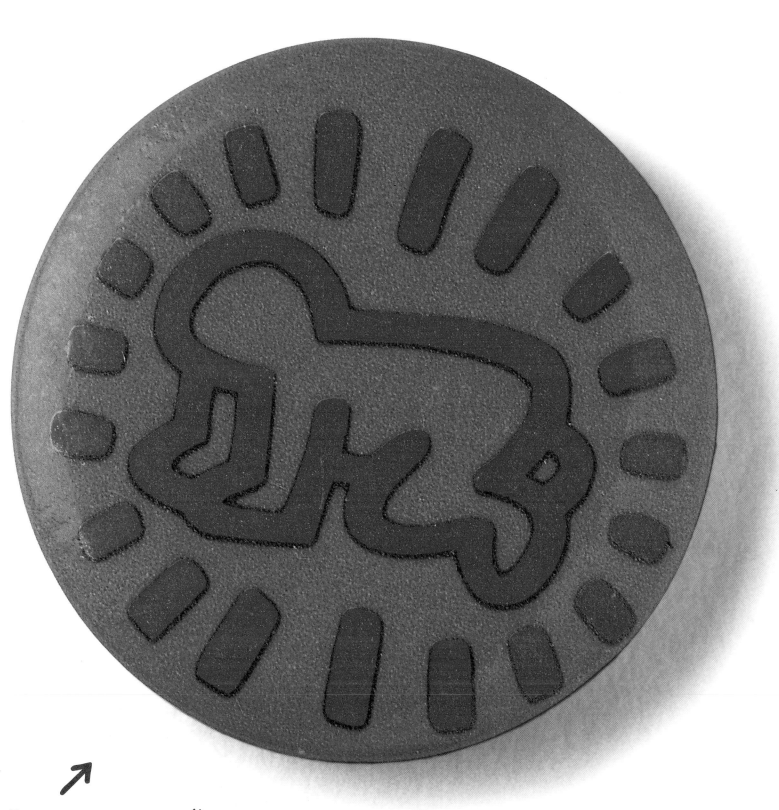

"RADIANT BABY"

STORIES

Once upon a time . . . Haring's first drawings were comics. He always had a talent for telling stories with pictures. Simple lines and symbols can mean so many different things. What's happening here?

I think in this picture these are poisonous flowers and they have died. They were cut off by a good person who realized they were bad flowers.

Who would tear off the flowers for no reason and just leave them on the floor? That's bad manners!

It was a hurricane.

I think this person is very pessimistic and when he got the flowers he cut off the pretty part and just left the stems.

What do you think happened?

I see a radio and the people don't like what they're hearing on the radio so they cut the wire.

They're putting people through this thing.

How do you know he's putting him in the machine? I think he's taking him out of it.

It looks like those kids have been kidnapped and this guy is getting them out. Out of that big machine that they're in. And he is pulling them out and they look very scared like they're trying to get out of the evil place. And then the wire— it looks like they're cutting the wire off the machine—the machine is broken. He seems to be checking if the machine is working or if it has stopped.

What story do you see?

MORE STORIES

He took a tea cup, a really big tea cup,
and cut two holes through it.

I think this person is very big and tough on the
outside and on the inside he's all weak and he's
very sensitive and he has a lot of feelings.

He has a really big big big butt! Humongous!

It's a Jack in the Box.

OK. There's this guy and he goes to the store to
buy a pair of pants. He likes all three of them and
the salesman says: "Buy them all" and so he does.

What do you think is going on?

EMOTIONS

Joy, love, excitement, anger, confusion, sadness. We all feel different emotions at different times. Can you tell how the people in the artwork feel? Sometimes the artist expresses how he feels through the use of pictures. You may feel certain emotions when you look at pictures.

They're at the doctor's getting x-rayed.

Maybe it's just a toy and these are the kids.

He feels betrayed by the world! Betrayed by his own feelings. I don't think he feels very good about himself. They're pulling out all his feelings.

How does this make you feel?

It looks like a snake.

He puts his hand through his body,
maybe to catch his brain.

He didn't want to be smart.

He doesn't like himself anymore and
he pushes out his brain and his heart.

I think this is a person who's all confused
and has mixed emotions. Someone hurt him
emotionally—someone hit him in his brain
and he's not good at math.

Maybe he's trying to reach for some love.

Do you ever feel this way?

MORE EMOTIONS

It looks like he's doing the 'moon-walk'.

He's using his sticks to drum on his belly.

This is a guy who has just broken up with his girlfriend and he's really angry with himself and he breaks his heart that looks like a stick.

This looks like a brick wall and this person has climbed all the way to the top and he feels mad and sad because he feels love has been circled out of his life.

Someone has died. See the cross in the corner. And he loved her. He's letting out his anger.

Which emotions do you feel from this painting?

MORE EMOTIONS

This is a big, old, slumpy giant.

I think this person is young,
but feels very old and weak.

He's a monster with lollipop eyes.

There are all these plus signs around him.
Like, improve your life! They're taunting him.

What do you think he is feeling?

TEAMWORK

Working together is sometimes the best way to get a job done. Everybody has different abilities and interests. People working as a team sometimes resemble a big machine and each person is like a different part of the machine.

I like the people because they look like they're all stuck together and they're dancing and jumping and playing tug-of-war.

This doesn't look like teamwork at all.
It's a pyramid of men.

These are acrobats from the circus. I can see a fat lady in the middle with two little clowns on her arms. The three blue men are fighting and the green man is the strongest man in the world because he can hold up all of the acrobats.

It looks like there are a lot people in charge here, and those guys with the x's on them don't mean a lot to society.

What kind of team do you see?

IMAGINATION

Sometimes we think of situations that are not real but excite our imagination. You can bring your imagination to life by making a picture, writing a song, or creating a dance. Everyone expresses his imagination differently and each person has his own unique story to tell.

I think this is a pyramid and these two
flying saucers are attacking a lady's house.
So she runs out and screams for help.

It looks like she's pregnant.

And the flying saucers are taking over her house
and everything, and she has to protect her baby.

I think this is a lady who is naked and just
when she was getting into the shower two
spaceships took off and she ran out of the
house to say "Stop it, you idiots!"

What do you imagine is going on?

MORE IMAGINATION

This man is sitting in his bath tub
and he's fishing for his dinner.

It's a guy that really smells so bad and he tries
to find out why. He lifts up his arm and he finds
lots of little fish in his armpit and he takes
them out.

He has gills on his ribs.

What do you imagine he's doing?

HAVING FUN - CELEBRATING LIFE

Playing around like a troupe of monkeys in a tree. Jumping around and laughing because life's so much fun. Learning to like yourself for who you are, and to like others because they are different and fun in their own way. Enjoying friends and life is a reason to celebrate.

It actually looks like a celebration 'cause they've got their favorite monkeys on the tree.

The tree has the measles and the monkeys are shaking it so the measles fall off!

It looks like they're doing frisbee practice with their halos.

I think the pink animals sort of look like fairies who come in winter because they're taking away all the leaves and filling up the tree with emptiness.

What do you think they're celebrating?

Front Cover:
The Story of Red and Blue, 1989
Lithograph, 22 x 16 1/2 inches
©The Estate of Keith Haring

Back Cover:
The Story of Red and Blue, 1989
Lithograph, 22 x 16 1/2 inches
©The Estate of Keith Haring

Keith Haring, 1984
Photo Tseng Kwong Chi
©1984 The Estate of Tseng Kwong Chi
and Estate of Keith Haring

The following pictures and photographs are listed
in the order of their appearence

Keith Haring in the subway, 1982
Photo Tseng Kwong Chi
©1982 The Estate of Tseng Kwong Chi
and Estate of Keith Haring

Button design, 1983
©The Estate of Keith Haring
Photo Nikolas Koenig

Untitled, January 5, 1989
Acrylic on canvas, 24 x 36 inches
©The Estate of Keith Haring

Pop Shop Quad III, 1989
Silkscreen, 27 x 33 inches
©The Estate of Keith Haring

Untitled, 1989
Silkscreen, 30 x 20 3/4 inches
©The Estate of Keith Haring

Untitled, October 3, 1987
Marker on paper, 11 5/8 x 15 3/8 inches
©The Estate of Keith Haring

Untitled, April 1985
Acrylic on canvas, 60 x 60 inches
©The Estate of Keith Haring

Untitled, 1984
Acrylic on canvas, 94 x 94 inches
©The Estate of Keith Haring

Untitled, October 1982
Vinyl paint on vinyl tarp, 72 x 72 inches
©The Estate of Keith Haring

Untitled, March 15, 1988
Sumi ink on paper, 12 3/4 x 19 1/2 inches
©The Estate of Keith Haring

Portrait of Andy, September 1984
Acrylic on canvas, 60 x 60 inches
©The Estate of Keith Haring

Untitled, 1985
Silkscreen, 23 1/2 x 31 inches
©The Estate of Keith Haring

Untitled, 1983
Silkscreen, 42 x 50 inches
©The Estate of Keith Haring

Untitled, 1980
Marker on paper, 14 x 17 inches
©The Estate of Keith Haring

Untitled (from *The Valley*), 1989
Etching, 14 1/2 x 12 1/2 inches
©The Estate of Keith Haring

The Tree of Monkeys, September 1984
Acrylic on canvas, 60 x 60 inches
©The Estate of Keith Haring

Self-portrait, November 6, 1985
Acrylic on canvas, 48 x 48 inches
©The Estate of Keith Haring

CONCEPT: DÉSIRÉE LA VALETTE, DAVID STARK
EDITORIAL AND DESIGN COORDINATION: CÉCILE HOHENLOHE
TEXT: GERDT FEHRLE, ADDITIONAL EDITS BY JULIA GRUEN AND LAURA WILSON
PHOTO RESEARCH: ULRIK TROJABORG

Children's comments to the pictures were recorded by Désirée la Valette
and transcribed by Taleen Gregerian:

5-YEAR OLDS, GRACE CHURCH SCHOOL, NEW YORK
Mr. Rich Carroll

David Balme	Syrie Bianco
Hilary Brashear	Calvin Brett
Carl Dawson	Suzanne Dirks
Hayley Doner	Devon Head
Kevin Kwok	Christopher Lange
Jack Langerman	Alexandra Marquis
Alexandra McClure	Samuel McCormick
Lorcan McGonigle	Samantha Mullen
Lillian Reape	Isabel Stillman
Allegra Tansey	Julian te Neues
Austin Wright	

8-YEAR OLDS, PUBLIC SCHOOL 116, NEW YORK
Mrs. Judith Ivry

Asa Ivry-Block	Emma Barnett
Elijah Rosello	Mariam Khan
Kemal Ugur	

12-YEAR OLDS, GRACE CHURCH SCHOOL, NEW YORK
Paz de la Huerta   Andrea Marpillero-Colomina

15-YEAR OLDS, UNITED NATIONS SCHOOL, NEW YORK
Maximilian Canepa
Stephan Linden   Cecilia Molinari

Library of Congress Cataloging-in-Publication
Haring. Keith.
Keith Haring : I wish I didn't have to sleep.
p.   cm   – – (Adventures in art)
Summary: Presents information about the modern American artist.
Keith Haring, along with a number of his pictures accompanied by "stories" about what they
ISBN 3-7913-1815-2 (hardcover : alk. paper)
1. Haring, Keith– –Themes. motives– –Juvenile literature.
[Haring. Keith– –Criticism and Interpretation. 2. Artists.
3. Afro–Americans– –Biography.]   I. Series
N6537. H348A4 1997a
709' .2– –dc21   97-2950
CIP   AC

Prestel-Verlag
Mandlstraße 26, 80802 Munich, Germany
Tel. (+49-89) 38 17 09-0; Fax (+49-89) 38 17 09-35
and 16 West 22nd Street, New York, NY 10010, USA
Tel. (212) 627-8199; Fax (212) 627-9866

Prestel books are availabe worldwide.
Please contact your nearest bookseller or write to either
of the above addresses for information concerning your local distributor.

Designed by Richard Pandiscio, New York
Production by WIGEL, Munich
Lithography by ReproLine, Munich
Printed by Aumüller Druck KG, Regensburg
Bound by Conzella, Pfarrkirchen

ISBN 3-7913-1815-2
Printed on acid-free paper